This copy of "Generations: A Japanese American Community Portrait" is a gift to commemorate the 100th Anniversary of San Francisco's Japantown in the Western Addition

The Japanese Cultural and Community Center of Northern California
1840 Sutter Street · San Francisco, CA 94115
P: 415-567-5505   ·   F: 415-567-4222   ·   www.jccccnc.org

Funding provided by the California Civil Liberties Public Education Program and
the Japanese Cultural and Community Center of Northern California

GENERATIONS

A Japanese American Community Portrait

Japanese Cultural and Community Center of Northern California

Editor:	Diane Yen-Mei Wong
Writing Team	
Coordinator:	Wendy Tokuda
Photography Editor:	Brad Shirakawa
Design Team:	Kurt Osaki, Nancy Ogami, Hats Aizawa
Project Director:	Paul Osaki
Project Coordinator:	Dori Takeshita

First Edition,2000

Library of Congress Catalog Card No. 98-075036

Generations: A Japanese American Community Portrait
Published by the Japanese Cultural and Community Center
of Northern California — 1st ed.

ISBN 0-9676601-0-6

Printed in Japan

C O N T E N T S

PREFACE

This project represents the culmination of many hours of meetings, discussions – some heated – and solo work behind a camera or in front of a computer. A team of writers, designers, photographers, researchers and support staff all came together to work on this photographic essay about Japantown's history and future. With so many talented, strong-willed people, decisions over photos, layout and format became tough judgment calls about how best to tell the story of a community that is still changing.

Each new contact brought us more photos and stories. Each session brought us closer to what we thought should be in the book. In the end, we reluctantly agreed that the book could never be totally inclusive but it could be representative of Japantown.

We thank everyone who contributed photos and shared memories, and who otherwise participated in the making of this book. A few people deserve special recognition for their work:

Kurt Osaki, Nancy Ogami and Hats Aizawa for working on the beautiful design and laying out draft after draft, especially as we continued to change our minds over the months.

Brad Shirakawa, for heading up the team of shooters and remaining calm in the face of machinations about each photo and for his willingness to go out time and time again to shoot.

Dori Takeshita, for collecting photos and working with families, archives and other collections and for staying with the project even after she moved on to another full time job.

Wendy Tokuda, for bringing in her tireless enthusiasm and professional journalistic perspective and for recruiting a great pool of Japanese American writers.

Paul Osaki, for the overall vision of the project, for keeping us focused on what the book was about, and for giving all of us a chance to contribute to this important effort to record a part of Japantown's story.

Thank you, Wen and Paul, for asking me to be a part of this wonderful book project.

Diane Yen-Mei Wong, Editor,
Generation: A Japanese American
Community Portrait

In 1998, while working on the plans for the 25th anniversary celebration of the Japanese Cultural & Community Center of Northern California (JCCCNC), I realized that the photos we had in our files told a story not only of the Center but of our entire community – its past, its present and its dreams.

Through those photos, I could see the soul of our community, and I wanted to give that soul a voice, so that even a child who could not yet read, and generations not yet born, could go through the book and understand what makes Japantown so special. They'll want to know who these people are, what they accomplished and why they kept pushing on despite the hardships. And in some small way, I hope that this book will help answer those questions.

The Center represents not only the struggle and triumph of the Japanese American community to build a home that it could call its own and that could never be taken away from it again. The Center also is a concrete symbol of how a community came together to build a permanent legacy for generations to come. The story of the JCCCNC is about the people of the community, the businesses, the organizations and hundreds of individuals and families who gave of their time, talent and resources to make the vision of the Center a reality.

It is this story of dreams and this story of our community that we wanted to share.

Everyday our community seems to be changing: a sign on a building, a storefront gone, a familiar face no longer there to say hello. Everyday a memory is forgotten, a story lost.

In some ways, our naivete enabled us to undertake this massive book project. If we had sat down to think about it, we might have concluded that we didn't have the time, experience or adequate resources to undertake such a huge project. But, just as in building a community center or an entire community, sometimes the vision takes hold and grabs you and will not let go until you give it life.

Many people shared family stories that illustrate what it took to make San Francisco's Japantown the first in the nation and to foster its growth in the light of great challenges such as racism, war, redevelopment, demographic changes and geographic dispersion. The Issei came to America with nothing but hope and dreams in their hearts, yet they thought of everything a community would need for generations to come: churches, businesses, schools, social clubs, families. And the Nisei continued to build upon that dream.

Ultimately, this book is about the generations that make up our community – you, me, all of us – and about who we are, why we are and how we all are parts of its long history and future.

We can pick up this book and see how the community established itself, grew and fought for its existence, and we can also get a glimpse of what the future may hold for Japantown.

When we finally paid off and burned the center's mortgage in 1996, many people who had been with us from the very beginning were no longer here. This photographic history will keep their memories and our legacy alive.

This is a never-ending story. None of us know what the ending will be, but one thing is sure: we will work hard to ensure that the roots planted by the Issei and Nisei will remain strong for generations to come. This is our challenge and our promise.

Paul Osaki, Executive Director, Japanese Cultural & Community Center of Northern California

1 | T H E   D R E A M E R S

In a 19th century Japan just awakening to the modern world, they heard tales of a veritable paradise across the Pacific. The pull was irresistible. Ahead of them lay adventure and the promise of striking it rich; behind them, bankrupting land taxes and a military draft hungry for sons.

In a trickle, then a steady stream, they crossed the ocean — some 380,000 strong. Most headed for Hawaii's sugar plantations, but 180,000 sailed directly to San Francisco, bustling gateway to America. They formed the first urban settlement of Japanese in this country.

The earliest of these new San Franciscans were a few thousand penurious male students who dwelt in sooty South of Market basements. They eked out a precarious living as domestic "schoolboys" in white homes while learning English.

They were soon joined, however, by thousands of male contract laborers seeking work in agriculture, railroads, mining and fish canneries up and down the West Coast.

From their first steps ashore, racism and hostility dogged them. In the way of dreamers everywhere, though, they made do — even thrived, settling in places that tolerated them: South of Market, Chinatown, South Park and later, the Western Addition, which became the permanent Japanese Town.

To feed, clothe and attend to them, a bustling network of commerce sprang up. By 1900, there were 26 inns and boardinghouses, prime centers for recruiting laborers. In 1912, 41 Japanese-owned pool halls provided social havens from the hardships of labor. In this tumult, community institutions also formed, including four Japanese daily newspapers by 1890.

The most momentous development for this fledgling settlement, however, was the arrival of 23,000 "picture brides" from Japan between 1908 and 1921, women who would transform a sojourner population into a permanent community by giving birth to American children.

Ultimately, these dreamers from another land found redemption in their Nisei children, whose American blood assured the legacy of their immigrant parents.

– Annie Nakao

In the sprawling sand dunes of the Sunset District, Motomu Ishii, 9, (child in center in white shirt) sits with his Issei parents at a Kenjin-Kai, or prefectural association, picnic in 1919 or 1920. Picnics often provided a sense of community and were well attended by immigrants and their children, all dressed in their Sunday best.

Kamechiyo Takahashi's first glimpse of America on February 17, 1917, provoked her to utter, "I had never seen such a prison-like place as Angel Island." Between 1880 and 1921, thousands of "picture brides" like Takahashi emigrated from Japan as part of arranged marriages. Because few new immigrants could afford to go back to Japan to marry, relatives, with the help of matchmakers, found brides for them and sent the women to America. Disembarking at Angel Island Immigration Station, these women endured bleak conditions, only to be released to husbands they had never met. Their courage and strength, however, led them to set down roots that transformed an immigrant society into a permanent community.

Crossing the Pacific to an unknown land, Japanese immigrants faced another hurdle upon arrival. At Angel Island Immigration Station, they were processed or detained for weeks, months, even years, if they could not immediately pass harsh examinations by immigration inspectors and doctors. Here, a panel of inspectors questions an immigrant.

South Park in 1920 was a bustling commercial strip. The Omiya Hotel and the Biwako Baths were among the businesses located here after the 1906 quake. A stone's throw from Piers 34 and 36, where ships from Japan docked, they enjoyed a thriving trade with crews and passengers.

South Park's Hotel Bo-Chow catered to the immediate needs of new immigrants as they departed from nearby piers. Typical of early establishments that grew to support Japanese students and seamen, the hotel was located upstairs from a *nandemo-ya*, or general store, that provided imported and domestic goods, as well as panoramic view finders and *omiyage* to send to family back home. The hotel co-owner was Shokichi Morino (c. 1910).

Legend has it that Takezawa Shiota immigrated to the United States with a dream of studying the art of perfume making. What he found instead was a niche for importing jade, porcelain, pottery and wood-block prints from China and Japan and selling these goods to a largely Caucasian market. The original store stood at 405 Dupont Street, along the borders of Chinatown, convenient to the upper class customers living in nearby Pacific Heights.

This mid-1920s photo shows Aki Hotel manager Mr. Goto at the wheel.

A group of students established the Japanese Gospel Society in 1877. The first Japanese organization in the United States, it served as a shelter and social gathering place for new arrivals and was the mother church to Japanese Christian churches that followed.

The very first Japanese baseball team on the U.S. mainland was the Fuji Club, founded in 1903, by Chiura Obata (far right). Obata, who later became a UC Berkeley art professor, was inspired to start the team after watching a pitcher from Waseda University lob snake balls at Stanford University's team. "This baseball game left an impression on me. I thought it was a good sport for young people," he said.

The club disbanded in the 1930s, but Obata's son Gyo continues the family's baseball tradition as a principal in Hellmuth, Obata & Kassabaum, Inc., the architectural firm that developed Pac Bell Park, Camden Yards, Coors Field and other well-known ball parks.

One of the most enterprising and successful Issei to arrive in San Francisco was Makoto Hagiwara, who was hired to maintain the elaborately landscaped Japanese Tea Garden in Golden Gate Park. Built for public exhibition at the 1894 Midwinter Fair, the garden boasted stone lanterns, bamboo hoop fences and teahouses in which *kimono*-clad Hagiwara family members served tea. Hagiwara's supervisory role lasted from roughly 1895 to just before WWII, except for a few years in the early 1900s, when an all-Caucasian Golden Gate Park Commission board rescinded the arrangement.

Temporary eviction in the early 1900s from the two-story Tea Garden exhibition house led the Hagiwara family across the street to 8th and Lincoln. There, Makoto Hagiwara began construction of his own "Japanese Village," complete with red *torii* entrance gates, traditional thatched buildings and ponds stocked with imported storks and fancy *koi*.

When the 1906 earthquake left Japanese residents homeless and in despair, the site served another purpose. Learning of the well-water supply and ample warehouse space, dozens of Japanese earth-

2 | OUR HOME

Japanese Town was home. It was a place where you could walk day or night and always feel safe. Roy Abbey fondly remembered its small town atmosphere. "The merchants, each one of them, would bring their brooms out and sweep to clean up the place." And when you strolled along Post Street to do your daily business, "We would say 'good morning' to everyone."

This was the Japantown that sprang up after the Great Earthquake of 1906, and reached its peak of activity in the late 1930s. "This is where we went to church, Boy Scouts, everything," recalled Joe Tondo. It was teeming with over four hundred Japanese-owned businesses. It was a self-contained community where all of your daily necessities and activities could be found.

"We weren't welcome anywhere else," Tondo stated. "In Japantown we felt comfortable." Here was the one place where you could start a business, begin a family, participate in a shared community life — all without concerns about discrimination and prejudice. Here was the one place you could live as a Japanese American and know it was just a normal way of life.

It was a vital community that was prospering economically and politically, a place full of hope, belief and future. As Tondo put it, "Japantown was everything."

– Philip Kan Gotanda

Looking west at Japanese Town, down the 1600 block of Post Street,

between Laguna and Buchanan Streets.

Kitaichi Sakai (center in dark vest) and three of his employees admire a premium catch in front of his Geary Street business, Uoki Fish Market, around 1910. Sakai later moved the shop to a rambling Victorian on Post Street, where he and his wife raised nine children upstairs. The store is still on Post Street and is run by Sakai's grandson Robert.

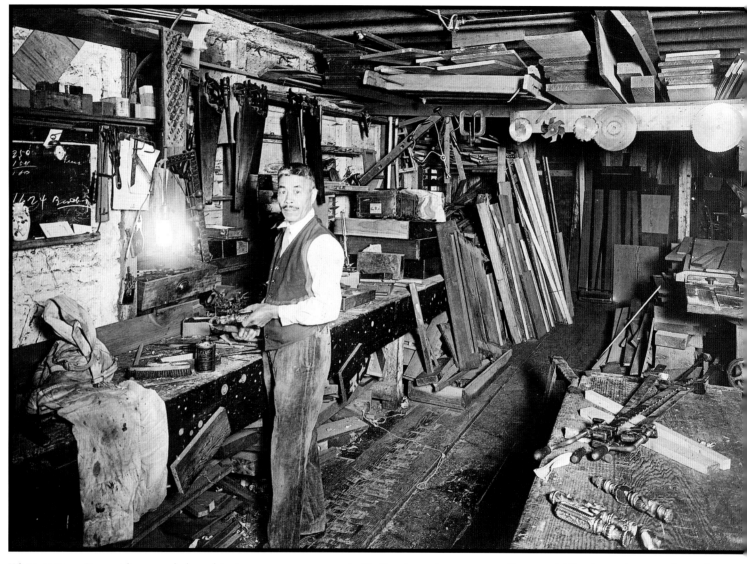

When community members needed a cabinet — or even a gym — built, they turned to carpenter Yasutaro Ishii, whose shop was located in the basement of a house on Post Street, between Buchanan and Laguna.

Every community had a soda fountain, and Japantown was no exception. Matsuya, located on Post Street, sold ice cream, homemade *manju*, cookies and *sembei* imported from Japan, and American cigarettes and cigars. This photo shows owner Yasutaro (right), his son Katao (center) and an unidentified employee.

The Goshado Bookstore, run by Shoroku Ono and Kanemitsu Aizawa (pictured) and located on the corner of Post and Buchanan Streets, was the only Japanese bookstore in the neighborhood in the early years. "Men dropped by my father's bookstore to talk politics or just to play *go*," recalled Aizawa's son Hats, "so there was always an aura of deep concentration. However, he didn't make it easy for these so-called intellectuals: they had to stand and use a countertop to play." Many dropped by after visiting nearby barbershops, "but they never bought," said Aizawa. "They just stood and read one-month old newspapers and magazines. They were all hungry for things to read in Japanese."

The Mikado Cafeteria was a family-run business from the early 1930s until May 1942. Operated by the Serata family (who also ran the adjoining Mikado Hotel on Post Street), the cafeteria had to be abandoned when the family was sent to the internment camp in Topaz, Utah.

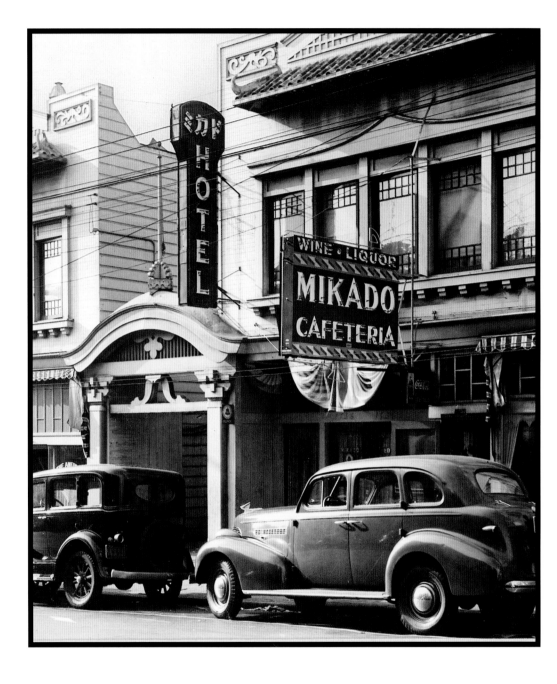

Former diners continually request the "recipe" for Mikado's famous fried noodle dish. According to the best recollection of family member Teiji Okuda, the dish included two to three scoops of white rice, topped with fried noodles, garnished with sliced roast pork or beef and green onions — all "drowned" in brown gravy. The price: 25 cents, with soup or salad an extra nickel.

In 1915, immigrant women wove their

way into the fabric of American life at

Tsuyo Tatsuno's sewing class, which was held

in the basement of her Buchanan Street home.

Tatsuno's son David recalled his mother was

"ahead of her time, because she wanted young

Issei to be self-sufficient in America by

knowing how to make their own clothes."

The Nichibei Bussan department store was a cornerstone for the growing San Francisco Japanese Town community. Shojiro Tatsuno opened the original store in 1902, near Chinatown, and moved several times before finally settling in at Buchanan and Post Streets in 1920.

Tatsuno was part of the fifth generation of family store owners in Japan but came to the United States to start his own shop. In the early days the store thrived because Tatsuno knew his community well, said son David. "Father knew Japanese didn't want to buy Japanese merchandise, so he sold Levis and other American clothing. I still remember seeing picture brides arriving in *kimonos* and leaving the store wearing ostrich hats and high button shoes. It was like they came in Japanese and left American." Later, when customers changed their buying preferences, the store specialized in Japanese goods. It closed in 1997.

Recalling to the Japantown of old, Lily Abiko said, "People knew each other better. And they knew what each other was doing. They knew where their fathers worked, where they lived, and what their mothers did. A lot of moms did bead work or embroidery work. A lot of the young fellows worked at Nippon Goldfish."

Lily Abiko

San Francisco hosted the 1915 Panama Pacific Exposition, which marked the opening of the Panama Canal. Japan had an exhibit at the fair and asked local Japanese businesses to participate in the parade if they wanted to. Nippon Goldfish owner, Tagayasu Murata, stepped forward and created a goldfish float, a sort of moving billboard. "My cousin's father was driving a car hidden under the fish and had a hard time driving the float, because he couldn't see," said Koji Murata.

Children loved to visit Nippon Goldfish and linger near the backyard pools, where the fish were raised and stored. Koji Murata remembered how they sometimes fell in and needed to be rescued. The store opened at this Buchanan and Sutter Streets site after the 1906 earthquake. In addition to goldfish, the shop sold *koi* and exotic fish, which it bred and shipped across the country. Handmade aquariums, welded by an ironworker from Japan, were another specialty. When asked how he made a living, owner Tagayasu Murata would reply that he had discovered how to extract gold from goldfish.

George's Candy Store, at Geary and Buchanan Streets, was the place to satisfy the sweet tooth in pre-war Japanese Town. Dapper George Ishizuka, Nancy Ono, George's wife Kiyo and Betty Kisera (left to right) preside over gleaming cases of handmade chocolates, peanut brittle and hard candies. The store closed after the evacuation in 1942.

Japanese Town in the 1920s was a residential community where the Issei settled and raised their families. Children, shown here on the steps of a Japanese-owned millinery shop on Buchanan Street, between Post and Sutter, made the streets their playground and enjoyed games like "kick the can" and "pee-wee."

Kaz Kataoka is shown here playing in the backyard of his family's home and business, the Aki Hotel, on Post Street. They could play ball on Buchanan as well, he said, because there was so little traffic. Kataoka remembers when only four Japanese Town families owned cars. "Everyday a popcorn vendor came by in a horse carriage," he said, and "every evening an iceman would come selling ice." He also recalled that some streetlights were lit by gas, and in the evening a man would come to light them. Life moved at a human pace back then.

The Ellen Stark Ford Fujin (Women's Home) was established under the missionary services of the Pine Methodist Church to shelter single mothers, orphans and children of broken homes. Girls up to the age of 16 were taken into the home. From there, white Methodist matrons, such as the one shown here in this 1912 photo, placed the girls mostly in Japanese foster and adoptive homes throughout San Francisco and oversaw how they were raised. Although children housed in this grand Victorian home were predominantly Japanese, Korean refugee children also stayed there.

Mr. and Mrs. Ichiro Kataoka pose with daughters Joanne (Sato) and Mary (Matsuno) on the corner of Post and Laguna. The girls, now adults, remembered how much Japanese Town was like a village in the 1930s. Everything you needed was close by.

In this photo, Maya Kataoka whose family owned the Aki Hotel celebrated her birthday. The chil-dren all wore hats that came in their party favors. At this same long table, Mrs. Kataoka served breakfast and dinner for some of the single men staying at the hotel.

昭和十一年五月二日
元岡摩耶子之誕生日満六才

31

Families walked to Dreamland (later known as Winterland) for the annual *sumo* tournament. There, they witnessed neighborhood boys transform themselves into *sumotori* in hopes of winning the coveted title and cash prizes. Charles Kikugawa (center), one of the mainstays of the popular event, went on to become a noted jazz musician.

Yoshiko Sano (third from right, back row) was a visionary leader who identified needs of the growing community. He helped to establish Nippon Gakuin, a Japanese language school located on Sutter Street, and the Japanese Boys Association, the forerunner to Boy Scout Troop 12, which formed in 1915. The troop survived the internment years and continues to serve boys in the community to this day, making it one of the oldest Boy Scout troops in the nation.

33

Shortly after the passage of the 1924 Immigration Act that ended immigration of Japanese because they were "aliens ineligible to citizenship," Congregational missionary and long-time advocate of Japan-US relations, Dr. Sidney Gulick, organized the Friendship Doll Exchange. In a goodwill gesture, almost 13,000 blue-eyed dolls collected from across the country were shipped to Japanese schools as "friendship ambassadors," and 58 Japanese dolls representing prefectures and major cities in Japan were sent to America.

This debut in San Francisco of the three-foot tall *torei ningyo* is believed to be the only display of all 58 dolls together. They were later ceremoniously presented to children across America and eventually found homes in museums and cultural institutions.

During the 1920s, young Issei women were not allowed to use other YWCA facilities. So, they raised money to buy property for one of their own and to construct the actual building at 1830 Sutter, between Buchanan and Webster Streets.

3-6

Hats Aizawa was a member of the Japanese American Marching Band. "The main players were capable and some, very talented," he said, "but more than half of us just put on a uniform and started learning. They hired one instructor, and he had to teach all of us. If you played second or third clarinet, you just had to play two notes, 'boom-pah, boom-pah.' Like that. The teacher must have gone crazy, now that I think about it. It's kind of funny now, but back then, we were really serious about it."

Hats Aizawa

dance class poses for a picture after a performance in Golden Gate Park, c. 1939.

In early 1942, the Tanforan we now know as a shopping center in San Bruno was a horse track frantically being converted into a concentration camp. Eight thousand people of Japanese descent from the Bay Area would be interned here for six months, while the Topaz Relocation Center was being built in Utah.

The crackdown in San Francisco actually began on December 7, 1941 — Pearl Harbor Day — when police officers and FBI agents swept down on Japantown, blocking it off, and arresting Issei community leaders. Before the police stepped in to prevent any possible violence, cars filled with the curious drove slowly through the neighborhood. "They just kept coming and coming . . . staring at us," said Yo Hironaka, who was just out of high school at the time. It scared her, and she remembered telling her friends they'd better go home.

About a month later, that cold fear entered her family's house on Geary Street. She returned one day to find her father gone, his office ransacked. In tears, her mother told her that the FBI had taken him away. Dependent on him for everything, her mother was never the same after he was gone.

The government orders came quickly – the curfew, then the order to evacuate. People rushed to sell everything they could but also made careful decisions about what to pack and bring with them.

Among those who reported to Kinmon Gakuen to be evacuated were Dr. John Hada, his father, and his 80-year old grandmother. They were disoriented and confused, and even though he was only 14, he recalled thinking, "Here I am a citizen of the United States, and I'm being hauled away by armed military personnel with bayonets. I couldn't understand why the government was treating us that way."

When they arrived at Tanforan, Dr. Hada cried when he saw the horse stall where they would live. He worried about his frail grandmother, who had raised him after his mother had passed away. The stables had no heat, and it was difficult for his grandmother to walk all the way across the racetrack to the mess hall for meals. The kindness of other internees who stopped by to check on her moved him. Dr. Hada's grandmother later died in Topaz.

The evacuation stopped life in its tracks for 120,000 people of Japanese descent on the West Coast. Most of them lost virtually everything they owned. The experience separated them from America – an experience so painful it would take a generation before they could even talk about it.

– Wendy Tokuda

Japanese Americans lined up as they arrived at Tanforan Assembly Center,
located about 13 miles south of San Francisco.

The April 1942 wartime evacuation of San Francisco's Japanese Town swept up women and children like 28-year old Fusaye Nakamoto, (upper step) who had two young children and was pregnant with a third. Right after Pearl Harbor, the FBI had rounded up her husband Jitsuzo, because as a storekeeper, he had once made a donation to a group in Japan.

"It was a hard time," said Nakamoto, now 85 and living in Japantown. "It's a good thing I didn't go crazy." She had to close up the family's Buchanan Street grocery store, the American Fish Market, by herself. "I had to sell everything."

The family went to Tanforan, then Tule Lake, California, and Topaz, Utah, where, 15 months later, Fusaye reunited with her family. Her only solace was being able to go to camp with her obstetrician, Dr. Kazue Togasaki, who aided many expectant mothers in camp. The Nakamoto's newborn son died in camp.

Here, on the steps of adjoining Japantown flats are (front) Shigeko Matsumoto, who also gave birth in camp, and (back, from left) Dr. Togasaki's niece Sachiko Yamanaka, 11; Helene Nakamoto (Mihara), 7; Mrs. Nakamoto; and Judy Nakamoto, 3. Below them is a posted evacuation notice.

FIRST S. F. JAPANESE PRISONER

安藝ホテル

START OF ROUNDUP—Ichiro Kataoka, } agents and San Francisco plainclothes-
owner of Aki Hotel, 1651 Post Street, } men yesterday as statewide crackdown

Seen in this *San Francisco Examiner* photo, Aki Hotel owner Ichiro Kataoka was one of the first Issei arrested in Japantown – within hours after Pearl Harbor was bombed. A Hiroshima prefecture banquet had been scheduled at the hotel that night, and scores of people were questioned for hours, boxes of documents seized.

His daughter Mary Matsuno, about 12 at the time, remembered her mother running after her father to give him a jacket in case it grew cold. Daughter Jeanne Sato said their mother also tried to cover the handcuffs with a handkerchief, so no one could see them. They would not see their father again for years.

Just before the internment, Nichibei Bussan held an "evacuation sale." David Tatsuno was running the store and recalled, "Our customers were mostly Japanese and didn't know how much to buy, because they didn't know what they'd be able to take to camp . . . We couldn't sell a lot of our merchandise, because prejudice was so heated nobody wanted it." Ironically, "as it turned out, when we were released, we were able to re-open the store, because we had so much stuff."

Katsuto Sakai is shown here boarding up the family store, Uoki Sakai, on April 4, 1942. His family owned the building on Post and lived upstairs, above the store. Not knowing what would happen to them, they sold all the perishables and put everything else in storage. Then they rolled the company truck and their old Dodge into the store and boarded it up. They were among the lucky: when they returned after the war, everything was intact.

With evacuation looming, many Japanese American business owners closed up shop. The Kisen Company, located in Chinatown, was forced to sell everything; it never reopened.

Buses also left from 1701 Van Ness Avenue. Evacuees were told to bring blankets, toiletries, clothing, plates, bowls, forks, knives and spoons. The War Relocation Authroity reported that "departure of the first large group of Japanese late yesterday was orderly, and generally, cheerful. Most of the evacuees seemed to feel they were going on a picnic, with only the one-time ever present cameras missing."

Confusion. Fear. Anxiety. All are captured in the face of this unidentified young man, waiting at 2020 Van Ness Avenue to be evacuated. He was one of 664 Japanese Americans in the first contingent to be taken from San Francisco on April 6, 1942. These early evacuees were removed from the northern and western waterfront parts of the city, near Fort Point and Ocean Beach. These areas were deemed sensitive for reasons of military security because of their proximity to the Presidio, an army base designated as the Western Defense Command Center during the war. The Tanforan Racetrack had not yet been converted to an assembly center, so these evacuees were sent to Santa Anita Assembly Center in Southern California, and later moved to Manzanar.

The government ordered heads of families to register for the evacuation at Kinmon Gakuen, a Japanese language school, on April 24, 1942.

Roy Abbey, then a young father, said, "We didn't know what to do, so we had to go along with the government. What could we do? We got our tags, our numbers . . . just like a prisoner." Even his six-month old baby received a tag with a number.

Another Nisei, Mary Matsuno, remembered how she felt when she got her number, saying, "I lost my name, my identity, who we are."

"We got our tags, our numbers . . . just like a prisoner."
– Roy Abbey

47

48

On April 29, 1942, buses arrived at Kinmon Gakuen, at 2301 Bush Street, to pick up one of the main contingents of evacuees and take them to the Tanforan Assembly Center.

From a government pamphlet, **Preparing for Relocation:**

Question:
What kind of clothes should I take with me when I am evacuated?

Answer:
Be prepared for the Relocation Center, which is a pioneer community. So bring clothes suited to pioneer life . . . Bring warm clothes even if you are going to a southern area, because temperatures may range from freezing in winter to 115 degrees during some periods of summer.

Roy Abbey remembered the confusion as he waited at Kinmon Gakuen to be evacuated. He and his wife had to carry suitcases for themselves, their four-year old daughter and six-month old baby boy. "They told us you cannot take more than what you can carry," he said, "so my wife and I went to the drugstore and bought medicine for the children, not knowing if they would have medicine or food for them. All that, plus blankets for the children. What else can you carry?"

In spring of 1942, bus after bus brought approximately 8,000 men, women and children to the Tanforan Assembly Center, which had been quickly transformed into a prison, with barbed wire crowning the chain-link fences to prevent escape and with armed guards in watch towers.

One internee, Ernie Iiyama, recalled how he felt when he saw the horse stall where his family would live. "The animal smell still lingered, and it had been whitewashed so quickly there were still horse hairs stuck in the paint. We would leave the door open because of the smell," he said.

Another Tanforan resident, Daisy Satoda, who was a teenager at the time, said, "It happened so fast, we didn't give much thought to it. We were just bewildered. What could we do?"

Tanforan had no classrooms for children or medical facilities, so Caucasian friends on the outside donated books, supplies and medicine to furnish schoolrooms, make-shift hospitals and eventually libraries, such as the one here. For many internees, camp libraries became a place of solace, a connection to the outside world.

TANFORAN ASSEMBLY CENTER – SAN BRUNO, CALIFORNIA
NOTICE
VISITING HOURS: 10:00 A.m. TO 12:00 noon – 1:00 P.m. TO 4:00 P.m.
VISITING AND OTHER CONTACTS DURING THE ABOVE HOURS ONLY
VISITORS SHOULD NOTIFY THE CENTER IN ADVANCE BY MAIL
ADDRESSED TO WILLIAM R. LAWSON CENTER MANAGER, TANFORAN
ASSEMBLY CENTER, SAN BRUNO, CALIFORNIA, GIVING DATE, PER-
SON TO BE CONTACTED AND PURPOSE OF VISIT.
    VISITORS PRIVATE CARS WILL NOT BE ALLOWED WITHIN THE GROUNDS.
    ALL PACKAGES AND PARCELS MUST BE LEFT AT THE INTERNAL
POLICE HEADQUARTERS ADJACENT TO THE MAIN GATE.
    VISITORS ARE REQUESTED NOT TO BRING FOODSTUFFS OR OTHER
PERISHABLES TO THE CENTER.
    PACKAGES AND OTHER PARCELS WILL BE EXCEPTED ONLY DURING
THE ESTABLISHED VISITING HOURS.
    ALL VISITING MUST BE DONE AT THE RECEPTION ROOM IN THE
MAIN BUILDING.
    VISITORS MUST LEAVE THE GROUNDS PROMPTLY BEFORE THE
END OF THE ESTABLISHED VISITING HOURS.
                    WILLIAM R. LAWSON
                    CENTER MANAGER.

NOT RESP
PACKAGES

54

In August 1945, Henri and Tomoye Takahashi stood on the deck of the ferry, cradling their two children born in the Topaz internment camp, staring at the approaching San Francisco skyline. "All of a sudden, we saw seagulls flying over the boat, like a gesture of welcome. We just stood there with tears in our eyes. We were so moved," remembered Tomoye. After three years behind barbed wire, they were home. At least in spirit.

Their house was filled with strangers sleeping in every room, relatives waiting for soldiers to return from the war. All their belongings – furniture, appliances, *kimonos*, ceremonial dolls – had been stolen. The Takahashis had left irreplaceable family photo albums with a neighbor for safekeeping. "When I went to pick them up, they told us they were so afraid of being labeled 'Jap lovers' they burned the pictures. That was devastating," said Tomoye.

Japanese Town had changed too. Virtually every building was crammed with African Americans who had flocked to San Francisco for wartime jobs, producing a severe housing shortage. Some Issei and Nisei found temporary shelter in what little space was available. Others scattered throughout the city.

Some things – like wartime hostility – had not changed, however. Japanese Americans were barred from swimming pools. Some restaurants refused to serve them. Banks turned down loan applications. Dr. William Kiyasu tried to obtain a student loan for medical school, but "they said we were too great a risk. We were still considered enemy aliens who might get shot."

"Nobody wanted to hire you," recalls Mas Kawaguchi. "They wouldn't even sell me a house."
In some ways, it seemed as though they were still in internment camps minus the barbed wire and guard towers. Still, in the midst of all the adversity, there were exceptional acts of kindness.

"We were blessed," says Sumi Honnami. Her family had left all their possessions with their African American landlord in Japantown, who not only returned them intact but had supported the Honnamis during their detention despite the risk of being tainted as giving aid and comfort to the "enemy."

Slowly, as the internees trickled back to San Francisco, Japanese stores and businesses began to reopen, but it would be years before Japantown would even begin to resemble the community they had been forced to abandon. Many started over with nothing but the determination to rebuild their lives and their community. In the end, they did just that.

– Ken Kashiwahara

Upon returning to the San Francisco Bay Area, many former internees found temporary homes in barracks, like these at Hunters Point on the bay.

Shown here is a community kitchen at one of the temporary resettlement centers to which San Francisco Bay Area's Japanese Americans returned after their release.

Honnami Taiedo reopened
as a "cubby-hole store" at
1630 Buchanan Street,
around November 1945,
making it one of the first to
come back after the war,
recalled daughter Sumi
Honnami. The store specialized in Mashiko ceramic
folk art from Japan.

Originally established in 1932 by Hikochi Shimamoto, the Shima Transfer and Draying Company's trucks served as a vital link between San Francisco docks and local Japanese businesses. After World War II, the family set up a makeshift shop at a small garage and helped many Japanese American families move back into Japantown.

Since opening its doors in 1923, the Pine Street Laundry provided both home and business for three generations of the Sugaya family. It was one of the first businesses to reopen after the war ended.

As Japanese Americans resettled, culture began to re-emerge. The Sokogeikai amateur *Kabuki* group first began performing in the internment camps and continued its performances at the San Francisco Buddhist Church and Morning Star School through the 1950s. Kinu Abe Matsumoto recalled how her mother and aunt helped dress her and other young women, assisting with elaborate costumes, wigs and make-up. Local *Kabuki* expert Mr. S. Ogomori, who did domestic work by day, directed the group.

June Uyeda Sugihara (center), remembered, "We used to have to memorize pages and pages of *Kabuki* dialogue, which we didn't even understand. So we would have to write it in *Romanji* or *katakana*, and my sister Elsie had a deep voice, so she always took the man's role."

Every August, paper lanterns lit up Buchanan Street between Post and Sutter for the annual Obon Festival, during which Buddhists paid homage to their ancestors. After many weeks of practice in the Buddhist Church gym, on Bon Odori night, dancers met at church for help in getting dressed and tying the *obi* sashes properly. Decked in *kimono, tabi* (Japanese socks) and *zoris*, they shuffled several blocks to Buchanan, where, like generations before them, they formed a circle

Every year the Kinmon Gakuen Japanese language school held a *gakugeikai*, or pageant, to showcase student talent. The program usually included speeches and short skits, all conducted in Japanese. Pictured here with two students is the school's principal, Mrs. Tomi Osaki. At its peak, as many as 250 students attended Kinmon's after-school and Saturday language classes.

Soko Gakuen, sponsored by the Buddhist Church, was the other main Japanese language school in San Francisco. Talent shows featuring singing, dancing, comedy and skits – all done in Japanese – helped raise funds for the school. This March 1951 photo features Joe Moriguchi (left) and John Kono in a skit involving an udon seller and customer.

Formed in 1956, the Shinsei (New Star) Band played primarily popular Japanese tunes but occasionally mixed in American dance numbers to appeal to the younger Nisei crowd. For a time, the band provided live music for the annual Obon Festivals around the Bay Area, headlined at Cherry Blossom Festivals and talent shows, and served as the "house band" whenever popular Japanese singers came to the Bay Area. This photo is from a performance at the Scottish Rite Center in May 1962. Dancers from the Hanayagi and Rokushige schools often performed along with the musicians and vocalists. After 26 years, the band broke up in 1982, a victim of the rising popularity of *karaoke*.

Pictured here are the 1949 Bay District Basketball Champions, the Gales. After returning from relocation camps, boys' basketball teams formed throughout California. The Gales may have been champs that year, but Gales' team member Nob Matsui admits the Protos were the best local team. "Everybody wanted to be on that team!" he said.

Teams formed in part, says one former player, as a "self-protection" society and because members didn't "want to grow apart." In this same year, the Gales and Protos decided they could play together and they formed the Hi-Fi (High Finance) Investment Club. Hi-Fi members still meet once every quarter to discuss finance and half a century of friendship.

In 1950, senior Keiji (Kaybo to his childhood friends) Shibata played running back for the Washington High School football team. "Tricky and fast" is how one friend remembered him, which explains his nickname "Cagey-Keiji." Classmates recalled that he was one of only two Japanese Americans on the team.

They called themselves the 'Arbees,' a name derived from the letters 'R-Bs,' which stood for Royal Blues, the color of the team shirts, which were sewn by the members themselves. Most agreed that the teams – which also included the Dots, Sparks and Clovettes – provided great social opportunities by hosting picnics, roller skating and ice skating parties and formal dances. One team even held an annual awards banquet at the Fairmont Hotel. While

Celebrities who played at George's Pool Hall during the 1960s made the place "respectable" and somewhat famous, said one player. Cartoonist, humorist and Japantown archivist Jack Matsuoka sketched this scene of the pool hall and remembered seeing Japanese wrestler Ricki Dozan "breaking" on one of the tables. Others recalled seeing baseball Giants stars Willie Mays and "Toothpick" Sam Jones and Golden State Warriors Wilt Chamberlain and Nate Thurman, all shooting at George's. Price to play back then? Ten cents a rack. The pool hall was located on Post at Buchanan, but during redevelopment the building was torn down and owner George Teraoka moved the pool hall to Geary Street.

Although the fishing club formed in the 1920s, it wasn't until after the war that the group began calling itself the Nisei Fishing Club. For the annual Thanksgiving Derby, held the Sunday prior to the holiday, contestants bring their catch to Marsh Dobashi's garage, where the fish are displayed on butcher paper with the fish's weight and the person's name chalked beside it, as shown in this photo of the 1964 event.

During the rest of the year, members go fishing regardless of weather. William Kyono remembered an incident from long ago when a group went fishing on a foggy day in the Sacramento Delta. The fog was so thick the fishermen were forced to walk single file, keeping physical contact with the person in front. When they reached their destination, they counted heads and realized they had lost the fellow at the end of the line. They heard him calling for help in the distance: he had fallen into a crevice and needed help to get out!

The San Francisco Buddhist Church, the oldest in the United States, celebrated its one hundredth anniversary in 1998. Throughout the decades, the talent and dedication of the Fujinkai ladies remained a constant. Whether it was a religious holiday, fundraising event or funeral reception, you could count on the women preparing delicious *sushi* (shown here, c. 1950) or other *gochiso*, or feast foods. Although individual cooks might disagree on what ingredients to include and in what amounts, they all agreed that everything not only had to taste good but be picture perfect as well.

Nisei members of the Veterans of Foreign Wars take a break during their three-day convention in 1955, hosted by San Francisco's Golden Gate Memorial Post #9879. "Our goal was to unite all the Nisei veterans," said Harry Tanabe, "to help those with war-related medical problems and to gain greater political power by demonstrating strength through numbers."

As important as Japanese culture was to many Nikkei families, for the most part, the Nisei saw themselves more as Americans, as evidenced by this photo of a group doing the "bunny hop." Various social clubs popular at the time – such as the Stinkers, Arbees, Barons, Frogs, Cardinals and Saranas – hosted different dances. Kashiwa Aizawa Hatamiya, a member of the Stinkers, said she and her friends formed their club while in the eighth grade, with Miss Toshi Koba as advisor. She recalled the dances fondly – the friendly competition between clubs in designing dance cards and the song "Dream" played as the last dance.

Their social lives in the 1950s remained primarily racially segregated. Interracial dating was still considered taboo, and although World War II had been over for a decade, Japanese Americans were still not widely accepted into the Caucasian social community.

The year was 1959; the day, January 11. Dorothy Oda is shown here on her way to marry Mas Yanase at the Buddhist Church in San Francisco. The smiles on the bride and bridesmaids, Chiz Shiro and Lillian Morioka (husband Aki Morioka is the driver and owner of the Buick), hide the tears shed the day before the wedding. Assured by San Francisco retail store Joseph Magnin that her wedding dress would arrive in time from New York, Dorothy was crushed to learn that her dress was stuck on a train in Utah. She got married in a sample dress from the store, hastily altered for her. Her own dress did arrive – a day after the ceremony.

In 1948, Kowji Fukuoka, 18, (left) and Yasukawa "Skinny" Suzuki, 17, stood in front of the Evergreen Cafe, a favorite teen hangout on Buchanan Street. They both agreed that the "look" from that period included the DA (duck's ass) hairstyle held together by thick "Three Roses" pomade, Levis – which Fukuoka says had to be rolled up at the ankles and rarely washed, white T-shirts and the "Eisenhower" jacket, shoes with extra soles and metal taps. More than 50 years later, Suzuki (who used to be almost six feet tall and weigh only 150 pounds) still has that padded shoulder "loafer" blazer in his closet, "but it doesn't fit," he said, because his nickname "Skinny" doesn't apply anymore.

In the busy post-war years, the Barons, a social and athletic club of Nisei in Japantown (members shown here in front of the Booker T. Washington Community Center), shared club jackets, basketball tournaments and picnics, and forged bonds that survive even today.

Speedway Meadows in San Francisco's Golden Gate Park was the setting for the annual community summer picnic. It didn't matter to which church or social club you belonged; the picnic was truly a Nikkei community event where old friends could catch up with each other. Families brought blankets and *bento* to the park and shared their food. Activities for the children included three-legged races, water balloon throws and other typically American games. The picnic coincided with the arrival of the Japanese training ship, an event that enabled the San Francisco Nikkei community to display its hospitality to Japanese marine cadets. June Uyeda Sugihara remembered one year when her parents invited ten sailors to their house for a home-cooked Japanese dinner.

In 1960, a large crowd waited outside Kinmon Gakuen for a glimpse of Japan's Crown Prince Akihito and Princess Michiko during their first visit of San Francisco. Ruby Murakami Hata, who was only eight at the time, remembered joining the crowd with her Girl Scout troop, but "there were so many people, I never got to see the Prince and Princess." After Japantown, the royal couple went to Sigmund Stern Grove for an official welcoming ceremony, where another contingent of Nikkei greeted them.

STOP THE DESTRUCTION AND
RDA, LET THE TENANTS STAY
OUR HISTORIC
JAPANESE

STOP the
DESTRUCTION
of
Nihonmachi
!!!

STOP
THE
DESTRUCTION
OF
NIHONMACHI

The 1960s brought turmoil to Japantown. A peace march swept from one end of the city through another in 1968, with protesters streaming down Geary Street and the neighborhoods of Nihonmachi. The spirit of activism remained long after the march ended, and it was rekindled in the 1970s, when city-directed redevelopment threatened whole blocks in the area.

The redevelopment agency's condemnation of buildings in the neighborhood caught many in the Japanese American community by surprise. Roy Abbey, now 94, remembered that he had to move his barbershop three times during redevelopment. "I felt like City Hall was just taking over. We were wondering what they were going to do to us . . . They had no reason to kick us out." During both the wartime evacuation and now redevelopment, his question was, "Why did they have to kick us out?"

CANE, the Committee Against Nihonmachi Eviction, whose membership eventually swelled to almost 300 members, formed in 1973 to raise community awareness and protest the evictions. Redevelopment rolled on but not without demands to "Stop the Destruction of Nihonmachi," or Japantown, as many people now called the area.

Unexpected benefits returned to the neighborhood as activists redirected much of their energy, passion and ideals toward establishing community-based groups serving the elderly, children, youths, newcomers and former World War II internees. Many of these groups still exist, some now with staff members who were not even born during the redevelopment struggles but who continue the work of keeping the community alive and thriving.

– Dean Takahashi

The Committee Against Nihonmachi Eviction fought unsuccessfully to save this three-story Victorian-style apartment building at 1531 Sutter Street. The site returned to the community in 1984, when it became Kimochi Home, a board-and-care facility for the elderly. Dogged protests "made the city realize that that site was too politically hot," said Steve Nakajo, founder and executive director of Kimochi, Inc. "That worked to the committee's advantage in negotiating to get that land for a project that would benefit the Japanese American community."

CITIZENS AGAINST NIHONMACHI EVICTION
UNITED WE STAND
DIVIDED WE FALL

This apartment building on the corner of Sutter and Buchanan Streets became a "symbol of change" for residents and small business owners in Japantown, said Glenn Omatsu (standing in front on left with fist raised). This photo was taken just after the last tenant had moved out. The building was torn down about a week later to make way for a hotel. The community – both young and old – began to see the Redevelopment Agency's mass evictions as a second forced evacuation.

As a young Sansei on the CANE coordinating committee, Carole Hayashino remembered how she felt as she watched the evictions of Issei and Nisei "These are people who already lost their homes during World War II, and here they are . . . They worked to rebuild their lives, and now they're being evicted a second time."

The Hokubei Hotel was one of the buildings that fell to the wrecking ball. Bo Yoshimura recalled that his father, owner Eji Yoshimura, was heartbroken about the fate of the hotel, which had about a dozen apartments housing sojourners such as Buddhist reverends. "The agency forced my father to sell the hotel for next to nothing," he said. "We had little choice, since if we refused, the city was going to condemn it. It hurt him deeply, but he decided to go take a picture as they were knocking it down." The site at Geary and Buchanan Streets is now a parking structure.

By the mid-1960s, the view looking southeast from Post Street was not a pretty one. Bulldozers had made short work of about half of Nihonmachi, mowing down numerous Victorian-style residences and storefronts to make way for what would become the Japan Trade Center. During those early redevelopment days, city officials consulted only property owners. "The residents and small business owners who were just retiring had no voice," said Hiko Shimamoto, who was living with his mother when they received a 30-day eviction notice from the Redevelopment Agency in 1972. He later became vice president of CANE.

Rev. Lloyd Wake, former pastor of the Pine United Methodist Church in Japantown, worked with many Sansei activists early in the movement. "There was a lot of energy and enthusiasm fueled by young folks coming out of [San Francisco] State College and the UC [Berkeley] student strikes," he said. "Their concern was to get back into the community." While many Nisei resisted progressive – and sometimes even radical – ideas, Wake tried to be supportive. "They needed to be heard."

Babe and Mary Morino had to rebuild their business after redevelopment if they wanted to stay in Japantown. "It was hard even to get a loan from the bank," said Babe. "We were struggling, because we were still re-building after the war. It would have been a struggle without redevelopment, but to do that on top of the war . . ."

The continuing war in Southeast Asia came home to Japantown in the form of a mile-long protest march that began downtown, stretched down Geary Street, and made its way to Golden Gate Park. Many anti-war activists, like Mickey Imura, who marched that day behind the banner of the Bay Area Asian Coalition Against the War, later redirected their organizing skills. "When the Vietnam War drew to an end, a lot of young people continued to do work in Japantown," said Imura. "We were taking pride in our identity."

Activists such as Sandy Ouye Mori and Steve Nakajo started Kimochi, Inc. in 1971, with their grandparents in mind. Sansei realized that mainstream services didn't work for the largely non-English-speaking Issei. Kimochi, Inc. provided Issei and older Nisei with meals, transportation and social services in their own language and with a sensitivity to the Japanese culture. Services expanded to include a lounge (shown here) and Kimochi Home, a board-and-care facility.

"Starting Kimochi, Inc. was a matter of trust," remembered Nakajo. "I mean, there I was, this 24-year old Sansei with hair down to my ass, with a goatee and shades, in my VW van, trying to drive these little Issei women home. But once they understood my intentions, my desire to organize this community, they allowed me in. After three weeks, Mrs. Abe finally said, 'Yes,' I could drive her home."

Two Sansei pioneers in "The Movement," Jeff Mori and Sandy Ouye Mori met working together in the community. For months, their early romance was one of the best-kept Japantown secrets. Sandy worked with the elderly, saying, "I was very close to my grandparents. I felt very strongly after I got my college degree that I should be doing something to help my own people."

Jeff worked with youths, saying, "It's an investment of time, from one generation to another. I stayed with young people, because a lot of people were patient with me when I was growing up.

Established in 1969, the Japanese Community Youth Council gave teenagers and children a voice and place to go after school. It started as an informal grassroots organization that spoke to the needs of a new, contemporary generation. "At first it was just an old building that redevelopment had emptied," remembered Johnny Nagano. "Nothing was in there, just empty rooms. I was sitting at the bus stop waiting for my friend when I got recruited to paint. From that day on, I started helping." In this photo from the 1970s, youth leaders supervise younger children attending a JCYC day camp.

Boku Kodama (top row, third from left) and Wes Senzaki (bottom row, left), who passed away in 1996, first met through their involvement with the Committee Against Nihonmachi Eviction. In 1976, the two artists, both of whom embraced "the philosophy that art was something that should be open to everyone," started the Japantown Art and Media workshop (JAM), said Kodama. "The focus of the workshop was . . . to provide art programs and a sense of community in a real geographical location, much like Kimochi, JCYC and Nihonmachi Little Friends [Preschool and After School Program]," he said.

[J]ust eight years old when he started going to the Japanese [C]ommunity Youth Council, Johnny Nagano remembered [w]hen people moved out of Japantown after redevelopment. [I was] lost," he said. "I didn't have many friends outside of [t]he community. I grew up with these friends forever, and [w]hen they left, I was lost. I didn't have anyone to hang out [w]ith. JCYC made up for that. It gave me a place to go after [s]chool and hang out."

During this time, the community also added a large, city-supported cultural event: the Cherry Blossom Festival. Japanese American veterans, who served in World War II, Korea and Vietnam, have led the annual Cherry Blossom Festival Grand Parade every year since the parade's inception in 1968. "it is our way of contributing to the Japanese American community," said Shig Miyamoto (second from left), "and to show how proud we are to have served our country."

Jon Osaki, now executive director of JCYC, marched in the parade for 10 years, beginning in the early 1980s as a Cub Scout and then as part of Boy Scout Troop 12. He said that though the troop's drum and bugle corps participated in many of the city's major parades, "Cherry Blossom was the most important performance of the year, because we played before our community. I recall getting a rush of adrenaline getting over the top of Post Street . . . There'd be a mass of people – friends, family and people you knew."

In this 1968 photo, members of Boy Scout Troop 12 made their way down Post Street, followed by Mayor Joe Alioto, who was Grand Marshall of the first Cherry Blossom parade.

A teacher of Japanese classical dance for over 50 years, Michiya Hanayagi (foreground) has appeared in every Cherry Blossom Parade since 1968.

The Taru Mikoshi signals the end

of the parade. This shrine,

modeled after an imperial design

and constructed of *sake* barrels,

is carried by one hundred young

men running in zigzag fashion to

spread good wishes and *sake* to

parade watchers.

Grand Master Seiichi Tanaka is credited with bringing the art of *taiko* to the United States in 1968, with
the establishment of the San Francisco Taiko Dojo. The *taiko* drum has been considered sacred in Japan
for generations. It was first used to drive away evil spirits from crops and later to give thanks for a
plentiful harvest. Today, *taiko* is played in festivals throughout Japan.

In the 1970s, some activists began to take a new, critical look at the forced relocation of Japanese Americans during WWII.

Edison Uno, pictured center at a meeting of the Pine United Methodist Church, has been called the "Father of Redress," the man who urged Japanese Americans and others to campaign for an official apology from the US government for the WWII internment of Japanese Americans. A Nisei professor of Asian American Studies at San Francisco State University, Uno was the first to teach a college class on internment. He drew criticism for referring to the camps as "concentration camps."

"At the time, he was very unpopular," said Jim Okutsu, Asian American Studies professor and director of the Edison Uno Institute at the university. Nevertheless, "he was a very articulate spokesman, a catalyst for change." Uno planted the seeds for redress but died in 1976, more than a decade before the official apology came.

Supporters of the Japanese Community Youth Council and other activists started a new, more youth-oriented festival in 1973. The Nihonmachi Street Fair, held each summer, is designed to bring together all elements of Japantown and to bring back people who have moved to other Bay Area neighborhoods. In this early photo, local band C.P. Salt entertains the crowd.

6 REDRESS

For Japanese Americans, redress was an intensely personal question, a searching of the soul. At the same time, redress was a mass catharsis, a public rite of passage that thrust Japanese Americans into history books.

Behind masks of middle-class respectability, Japanese Americans had nursed deep psychological wounds since the last camp barracks were torn down. Most proud Issei and Nisei never spoke of the internment, even to their own children.

Redress transformed that pain into a political movement. In the Bay Area, the idea of reparations was first mentioned publicly at the "Day of Remembrance," when more than a thousand Japanese Americans made a pilgrimage to what used to be the Tanforan Assembly Center.

In 1981 federal hearings were held around the country, and Nikkei stepped forward and talked openly about the evacuation and internment.

Japanese Americans demanded redress for the estimated $800 million to $8 billion in losses wreaked by the internment. Payments also would stand as a stark reminder that the United States should never again violate its Constitution because of racial hatred and wartime hysteria. After a decade-long fight for redress, Congress and the White House signed the Civil Liberties Act of 1988, which led to $1.2 billion – $20,000 each – for the 60,000 survivors of the camps.

Redress was more than a debate over money. It was a bold stand for justice and civil rights. And it was a badge of honor for Japanese Americans who regained their dignity. In the end, redress liberated the Nikkei from a painful past and uplifted an entire community. A new era had begun for Japanese America.

– Edward Iwata

During a 1990 ceremony in Japantown, 100-year old Issei Chio Mizuno (center) received her redress check. Back at her rest home, she asked her friend Tokiko Ushijima (right) why the government had given her this money. The friend told her, "America is apologizing to you for the internment." The old woman smiled and nodded, saying, "Why thank you very much. This makes me very happy."

The "Day of Remembrance" held at the Tanforan Shopping Center, on February 19, 1979, marked a turning point for the Japanese American community. More than a thousand Americans of Japanese descent gathered at what used to be the Tanforan Assembly Center, carried there by a caravan of autos stretching more than a mile long.

They commemorated the 1941 signing of Executive Order 9066, which had led to the WWII imprisonment there of many Bay Area Japanese Americans. One of the organizers, Carole Hayashino, remembered, "It wasn't a feeling of being victims." Instead, "it was the first time in the Bay Area, Japanese Americans talked so openly about the internment," she said. "It was the first step for the community to discover its voice."

"It was the first step for the community to discover its voice."

– Carole Hayashino

The Commission on Wartime Relocation and Internment of Civilians held hearings in 1981 in cities across the nation, including San Francisco. Hundreds of Japanese Americans bared their souls in public, as if a wall of silence had been torn down. Slowly, before hushed audiences and the glare of television lights, their stories unfolded – stories of hope and survival, of lives lost and dreams deferred.

Hiroshi Kashiwagi was one of the "No-No Boys," the famed anti-draft protesters who refused to answer "yes" to WW II military loyalty oaths. Now a playwright and librarian in San Francisco, he was a fiery young man in the 1940s. Why, he thought, should he go to war for Uncle Sam when the nation had imprisoned his people? The No-No Boys were shipped to a high-security camp guarded by tanks in Tule Lake, California. Many renounced their citizenship for several years. Decades later, Kashiwagi spoke at the San Francisco redress hearing (shown here). "Only recently," he said, "have I felt like a true American citizen."

"At first , I said 'no' to pleas that I get involved in the redress movement," said retired pediatrician Clifford Uyeda, "but at the time [1977], I was among the few people who had experience with running a national campaign." Uyeda eventually ended up chairing the campaign. "It was very divisive at first. One group wanted individual reparations; the other wanted just community redress. 'It should be both,' I said, because both suffered." And then there were those who said, "We've come so far, why stir up those bad feelings all over again?"

Uyeda's leadership proved critical in launching and guiding the redress campaign. "The Sansei were behind the campaign; it was our job to try to make the Nisei understand why both a restitution and apology were necessary," said Uyeda. "As an American citizen, if you do something wrong, there is a monetary fine; and 'I'm sorry' is not enough. You can say 'I'm sorry' today and take it all back tomorrow."

"All the sad stories just got to me. I knew then we had to win. We had to get redress passed."

– Sox Kitashima

Through her work with the National Coalition for Redress and Reparations, 80-year old community activist Sox Kitashima spoke out in public and led a letter-writing drive – herself folding letters and putting stamps on envelope after envelope at her kitchen table – that flooded Congress and the White House with thousands of mailings.

She had became a true redress believer at the Commission's San Francisco hearing. Seeing the auditorium full of Nikkei brought her to tears. "All the sad stories just got to me. I knew then we had to win. We had to get redress passed." When she and other coalition members began lobbying in 1984, they were as "green as green," remembered Kitashima, "but if we had given up, there would never have been a letter of apology and $20,000 [to each camp survivor].

His face could tell a thousand stories. Kiyoshi Yamashita, a 95-year old Issei man from Oakland, was born in late 19th century Japan. In his new land, the United States, he spent World War II in the Topaz Relocation Center, ringed by soldiers and barbed wire in the Utah desert. Here, Yamashita is one of six elderly Issei to receive the first round of redress checks during a 1990 ceremony in Japantown.

The redress movement included the heroic legal struggles of three retired Japanese American men – (standing, from left) Fred Korematsu, Gordon Hirabayashi and Min Yasui) shown here with their team of attorneys (seated, from left) Dale Minami, Donald Tamaki and Peter Irons. As young men, the three Nisei had challenged the legality of the World War II milltary evacuation order and curfew for Japanese Americans. They lost their test cases before the US Supreme Court and served prison time and probation.

In 1983, however, the elderly trio brought a legal action based on newly found evidence, requesting the courts to vacate their 40-year old convictions. The legal argument in their *coram nobis* petitions: Court rulings at the time were based on historically false War Department findings that there was a "military neccessity" for the mass incarceration of 120,000 Japanese Americans.

As a defiant Fred Korematsu put it at his San Francisco hearing, "The government should not be pardoning me; I should be pardoning the government." Federal judges agreed and eventually vacated all three cases.

Korematsu's lead attorney Minami remembered being so focused on his argument before Federal District Court Judge Marilyn Hall Patel that he didn't immediately grasp the impact of what had happened. As he was leaving the courtroom, however, Issei and Nisei came up one by one, with tears in their eyes.
"I realized then," he said, "we'd done something remarkable."

"I realized then we'd done something remarkable."

– Dale Minami

99

Japantown and its constant evolution symbolize the challenges of being Japanese American in today's society. With one foot planted in Japanese tradition and culture, the other foot is firmly planted in contemporary Japanese America, with Nikkeis looking for the balance in preserving their heritage with the changing face of the community.

The Issei memories of Japantown are those of inns, restaurants and pool halls. The Nisei remember the Evergreen Fountain, American Fish and Mike's Arco. All those sites are now gone.

The promise and the future of Japantown now rest in the hands of the younger generations. Their memories include images of street fairs and Cherry Blossom Festivals, meals at Iroha and Denny's, and shopping at Super Koyama or Sanrio. Their last names may be Lam or Zimmerman or Burton, but part of their hearts and souls will always be Japanese.

Japantown has become a sacred trust, born from the sweat and frustration of Issei, resurrected and nurtured by war-torn Nisei, and revived yet again by activist Sansei. It is a special legacy, preciously handed down from generation to generation, now ready for a new generation to preserve and protect it for the future.

– Dianne Fukami

Kagami Kai, a year-round *mochitsuki* group, demonstrates *mochi*-making at the annual Nihonmachi Street Fair. While pounding the rice, group members play *taiko* to provide a rhythmic beat for the workers.

101

Chris Hirano has fond memories of growing up in Japantown: "Playing sandlot baseball, where the bowling alley now is, with cardboard bases and a *sembei* tin cover for home plate; thinking we were the Japanese Little Rascals and building go-carts and racing them down Buchanan Street; getting a 'suicide soda' at Benkyodo, or, if I had luckily found a dollar in my pocket, an orange freeze at Evergreen's."

Chris Hirano

Fond memories: "Thinking we were the Japanese Little Rascals and building go-carts and racing them down Buchanan Street . . ."

– Chris Hirano

The Buchanan Mall between Post and Sutter Streets, serves as a major pedestrian walkway connecting neighborhood restaurants, shops and other services. With its concrete planters, stone and wooden benches and lanterns, the mall is a favorite gathering place to meet friends, as well as a place just to sit and relax.

Traditional Japanese cultural activities attract participants of all ages. Here, Shoko Higake Matsumoto (left) helps Crystel Takata-Hadley, 8, with the correct fingering during a *koto* lesson held at the Japanese Cultural and Community Center of Northern California. Matsumoto, who started playing *koto* when she was three years old, has taught at the Center as an artist-in-residence since 1997.

At a doll-making class offered by the Japanese Cultural and Community Center of Northern California, Shirley Garrison-Felker constructs a Meiji Fuzoku doll, which represents a young girl from the Meiji era. Made of *washi* paper, wire and cotton, finished dolls may stand about a foot tall.

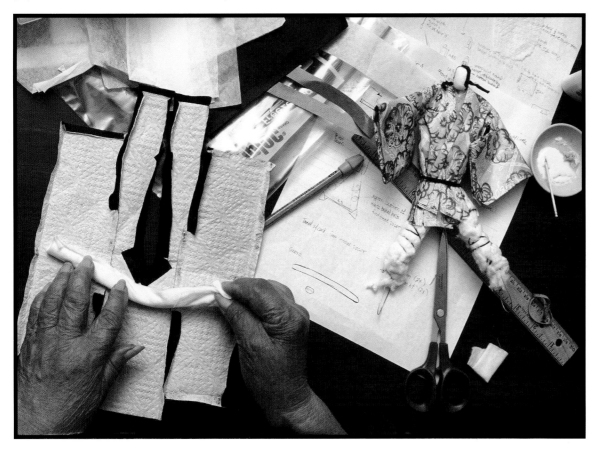

Six-year old Nanako Shimada, a recent immigrant from Tokyo, learns how to dance by watching adults participating at the San Francisco Buddhist Church's Obon Festival.

The drums began calling Susumu
Saiki when he was still a young man
in Tokyo. "I heard them beating and
walked four or five miles to the
Obon Festival," Saiki said. "A drum-
mer was beating a drum five or six
feet in diameter with a drumstick the
size of a baseball bat." After that
experience, he immersed himself in
learning the *taiko*-style drumming.
Almost 80, Saiki has become a fix-
ture at the Obon Festival ceremonies
for the Buddhist Church of San
Francisco – playing for more than
thirty years. "In a small way, I hope
my drumming keeps the Japanese
culture alive for posterity."

106

Roy Abbey (right) is shown here teaching pottery for Kimochi, Inc. He retired as a barber years ago and has volunteered at Kimochi for 22 years. "I really enjoy associating with the older people," he said, "because I myself am 94 years old now. When I see these older people staying home doing nothing, I think it's a shame. I'd rather see them socialize with other people, enjoy themselves and do whatever they can."

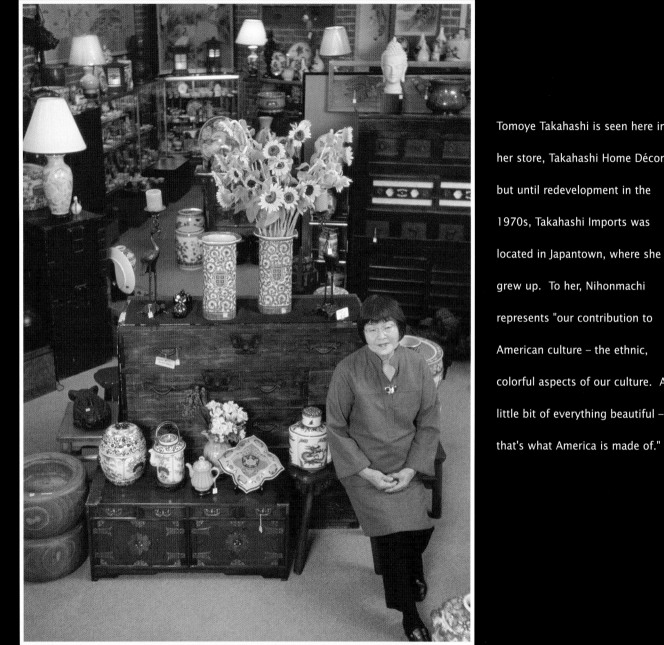

Tomoye Takahashi is seen here in her store, Takahashi Home Décor, but until redevelopment in the 1970s, Takahashi Imports was located in Japantown, where she grew up. To her, Nihonmachi represents "our contribution to American culture – the ethnic, colorful aspects of our culture. A little bit of everything beautiful – that's what America is made of."

Despite the challenges of the internment and redevelopment, several Japantown businesses survived and still operate as family affairs. Frank Takao owns and works at the Toraya Restaurant, which his father Yoshinori Takao started in 1965.

"I took my father's drive," he said. "He came from an era when success was defined by hard work. I've been doing this since I was in junior high."

Frank learned the finer points of sushi-making from chefs in Japan and also from his father, and uses these skills to create the food ordered by customers. "I love the people. I really enjoy them enjoying the Japanese food I've prepared and knowing that they appreciate and know the finer qualities of it."

Larry Nakamura (left) and his son Chip meet every week for lunch in Japantown. Larry opened a neighborhood dental practice over forty years ago, and Chip took over in 1988. "Dad was involved with his kids as well as the community,' said Chip. "He was our scoutmaster in the Buddhist Church and president of the Golden Gate Optimist Club. He always said, 'Don't take the easy way out,' and he never did."

Chip became a dentist because of his dad, but they stopped talking business over lunch a long time ago. "We talk about golf a lot" mused Chip. "He's still an interesting, righteous guy."

Allen Okamoto (right) checks real estate listings as his father Takeo looks on. Their family-run realty company, T. Okamoto and Co., has been in Japantown since 1947. "Initially, working with my father was hard," said Allen. "I was a college kid, and I thought I knew everything. Later, I realized I was *him*. We have the same belief system; he's honest and hardworking. He tried to instill all those good Nisei characteristics in me. I found my dad was a great teacher, and he's probably the most honest man that I know. He's 91, and he still comes in everyday."

Brothers Minoru and Kahn Yamada took over Jim's Drugs from their father. Kahn (right) doesn't remember wanting to be anything else other than a pharmacist, and it seemed natural that he and his brother would take over the drugstore that carried their father's name. "My dad had an easy chair in the back, and people would come back and talk to him," said Kahn. The neighborhood has changed now, but the store is still a family operation. "We spend a lot more time out in front with the customers whenever we can, instead of relegating it to a clerk. We like it to be personal."

Dr. Wilfred Hiura (left) and Dr. Pearce Hiura (right) founded their optometry practice in 1949 and have been at the same Polk Street location since that time. Active with several Japantown community groups, the two brothers were original planners of the Kimochi golf tournament. Dr. Ronald Hiura, son of Pearce, joined the practice in 1980 and now does the bulk of the work.

112

Ricky and Bobby Okamura run the family *manju* shop, Benkyodo, located right on the Buchanan Mall. Ricky, shown here, makes the *manju*, while Bobby works more out in front. "Although there are five of us kids, we were not pressured to take over the family business," said Bobby, "but it means a lot to Ricky and me to carry on this tradition. In a way, this is our way of serving the community, especially since making *manju* is a dying art."

Mas Ashizawa (right) and his son Phil, shown here with longtime employee Mrs. Nancy Tomioka, tend to the family-owned Soko Hardware store, located at Buchanan and Post. The store opened in 1925 and helped establish Japantown.

Mas took over from his parents in 1948, and led the community fight when the city tried to redevelop Japantown in the 1950s. "It was about self-preservation," said Mas. "The so-called redevelopment would have wiped out the Nihonmachi business.

Now third generation businessman Phil has expanded Soko Hardware to also sell Japanese imports and crafts. "We've co-evolved with the community," he observed.

114

George Okamoto, owner of Nomura & Company, remembered the early days of the business. "We did it all – growing it, milling it, distributing it," he said, describing the rice business his father-in-law began after World War II. "When we first started, we only sold rice in 100-pound bags. In the beginning, we knocked on doors trying to convince people that the medium grain rice we offered was better than the short grain pearl rice they were used to. I think they liked it once they tasted it." The company has donated sacks of rice to Kimochi for more than twenty years.

The designer behind many Japanese American buildings, including churches and the Japanese Cultural and Community Center of Northern California, Wayne Osaki tries to incorporate "some sort of Japanese feeling" in his projects. Talking about the neighborhood, he said, "It was mostly Victorian houses and buildings. Although it was Japantown, it didn't really have an atmosphere. I tried to bring some sense of identity – a sense of the Japanese cultural background so that people could feel comfortable."

Kaz Maniwa, shown here talking with Kimochi volunteer Sox Kitashima, helped establish the Japanese Community Youth Council in the 1970s. "We were naive and very idealistic, and we felt like the most important thing in the world to us was to build a strong community." That commitment led him to start his own law firm in Japantown, right after he graduated from law school.

"It's very special to be able to walk around the community and know most of the people in the area," said Maniwa. "It's kind of a country lawyer thing. When you've gone through deaths, births, marriages with people you see all the time, that links us. That's the glue. We have so much history together."

Moses Yasukochi owns Sweet Stop, a bakery located on Sutter at Buchanan. He has worked in Japantown for about twenty years, and he worries about its future. "I see the dwindling of the community, because there aren't as many Japanese business owners anymore," he said. "Their kids don't want to take over the family business. My oldest daughter works for H.P. [Hewlett-Packard]; my youngest daughter is a firefighter, and my other daughter is a registered nurse. I asked them, 'Do you want the business?' and they said, 'No way, Dad.' They see how hard the work is."

Joe Tondo (left) and Mike Inouye both started pumping gas and lubing cars as young men, straight out of military service, right after the war. Eventually Tondo owned Joe's Exxon on California Street, and Inouye owned Mike's Richfield on Pine. Both hired youths from Japantown to pump gas. "I saw a lot of Sanseis grow up and get their first cars," said Tondo. "They're all grown up now. All the kids who worked for me when they were in high school, they went to college and became something — doctors, pharmacists. I'm kind of proud of that."

118

Robert Sakai, seen here in the upstairs storeroom of the family grocery store, is a third generation business owner in Japantown. His grandfather first peddled fish from a horse and buggy before opening Uoki Sakai in a building in 1906. "For me and my family and brothers and cousins, it's kind of a touchstone," he said. "I think where I really see it is with my mom and aunt. People they've known all their life come in and, in a real gentle way, said 'hello.' If you're not looking , you miss it. It's very touching."

Over the years, some Nihonmachi businesses have shut down. Harold Iwamasa was owner of the now-closed Toyo Theater and Kokusai Theater, which were located at what is now the site of Denny's Restaurant. "Sure I miss the theater. I often think of it – my son Ronald used to run the projectors, and I was chief janitor. My daughter ran the front . . . Seiji Ozawa [music director for the Boston Symphony] was a regular customer. Saturday and Sunday, he'd be there. Every time we did a samurai trilogy, it'd be impossible to get a seat. The line would be all the way down by the bowling alley."

"Sure I miss the theater. I often think of it –
my son Ronald used to run the projectors, and I was chief janitor.
My daughter ran the front... "

– Harold Iwamasa

Yamada Seika opened its doors in 1963, and for more than 35 years, Yasunari Yamada (center) used techniques passed down through three generations of his family to make some of the finest *mochi* and *manju* in Japantown. Working twelve hours a day, six days a week, he painstakingly prepared the food by hand. "Maybe we should have gotten machines. I don't know," the 67-year old said jokingly. "Maybe we wouldn't have worked so many long hours."

The ability of Japanese Americans to succeed outside of the community has, in a way, stalled business growth in Japantown, he said. "Business owners are older today, and their children work for big corporations now instead of going into business here." When it came time for Yamada to think about retirement, he looked three years for someone to take over the store. "I couldn't find anyone. It was so sad." Yamada Seika closed its doors for the final time in 1999.

When Rumi Okabe and her husband Mitsufumi started Okabe Sports in the 1970s, "Japantown was a natural. Our friends were here, as well as all our business contacts." She added, "After a while as our business started to grow, we thought about moving down towards the airport, but it never happened. After thinking about it, we would be giving up so much—seeing our friends and eating Japanese food. We would just end up in Japantown everyday anyway." The Okabes, also owners of Pacific Leisure Management, are seen here sitting in the Buchanan Mall, just outside the sports shop, which closed in 1999.

121

Much of what keeps Nihonmachi vital and vibrant are the people – people like Bay Area Nisei pioneers Clem (right) and Shizu Oyama, who hug every morning to "start the day right." Daughter Patricia calls them the "Siamese Twins," because of their partnership that began in the 1940s, when Shizu worked as a nurse to support Clem's business ventures, which ranged from bean sprouts to imports before running a very successful medical supply business in San Francisco.

"Dad was a dreamer with a creative mind. He had patents on many inventions now used in various industries. But he's always said Mom's support made those dreams come true," Patricia remembered. "Mom stayed in the background. It was a very 'Japanese' relationship. Mom gave him guidance he didn't always know he was getting."

Members of the Barons, a club that began in the years after World War II, still meet today. As the "boys" hit age 60, they began holding their first birthday parties. Seen here are five Barons, all brothers: (from left) Koichi, Michisuke, Nobusuke, Hiroshi and Saburo Fukuda.

Hiro and Susan Shimamoto have lived their entire married lives – twenty-five years – in Japantown. Although from time to time they had spoken about leaving when their two children were born, they felt it was more important that they grew up with a "sense of community." "Karen and Scott know who and what they are," said Susan, "and I think the community enhanced that to a degree."

They would like to see their children – and someday their grandchildren – live in Japantown. They realize, however, that their children's lives may take them elsewhere and that skyrocketing housing costs may also prevent them from staying. "We have one house, and hopefully one of them will stay here," Susan said, "but the decision to stay is theirs to make."

"I'm sure that J-town is always going to be there," said Ron Kanzaki, owner of the now-closed Kanzaki's Lounge, a popular Night Club that was located upstairs, at the corner of Buchanan and Post (in background). One of the founders of the Nihonmachi Street Fair – he came up with the idea while standing at the very location shown here – Kanzaki said, "It's important to maintain community spirit and to maintain [J-town] for the younger Japanese Americans, so they have a sense of identity and can be proud of who they are and where they came from."

The Donahoe family embrace a mixed heritage that started when Sean and Pamela (Nunotani) met at UC Berkeley in the 1960s. Pamela recalled "some resistance from both families" but added, "ironically, I came to appreciate that fear of losing cultural identity. I made sure my three daughters retained a strong sense of being 'Japanese' by keeping them involved in the J-Town community. Fortunately, Sean was always supportive. In fact, if he weren't Irish, he'd be Japanese."

Daughter Erin added, "It makes me feel special. I'll go from an Obon to a Saint Patrick's Day party. I get more chances to celebrate 'who I am.'"

According to Rebecca Chiyoko, an assistant sociology professor at the University of San Francisco, the out-marriage rate in the Japanese American community is about 42 to 50 percent. King, who herself is racially mixed, said that this develop-ment has "changed the way people think about the content and criteria of the category 'Japanese American.' The Cherry Blosssom Queen contest is a good example. Some wanted to just stop having it rather than lower the blood quantum rules to allow mixed women to run. San Francisco changed the rules and accepts mixed race Japanese American women; Hawai'i didn't for a long time – until [1999]."

"When we were growing up," said Gail (Onishi) Mametsuka, "we attended the Pine [United] Methodist Church and went to Girl Scouts, day camp and festivals there. Oh, and to eat, of course." Though Mametsuka and her siblings now live in many different parts of San Francisco, they carry on the J-town tradition with their children. "For us, there are role models there with interesting careers and histories. It's where we know we'll find cultural activities for them and where they'll feel a connection to their heritage. . . Now our kids go to day camp and participate in basketball and go to the church."

Mametsuka said, "Japantown is where we found our identity, where we found our spirit and soul in being Asian. It was a safe place to be who we were."

In this photo, the Onishi siblings and their families congregate at their mother's house in San Franisco's Sunset District to celebrate a birthday. "Not a day goes by that our lives are not connected in some way."

World famous artist, Ruth Asawa (seen here wearing hat) oversees the installation of one of her two "Origami Fountains" in the Buchanan Mall, in October 1999. The original fountains, of the same design, were installed almost 25 years earlier by the Redevelopment Agency, but they had to be turned off during the drought. They fell into disrepair and eventually had to be removed.

Asawa says she hopes the new fountains will help draw people to the plaza. She wants people to stop and enjoy them, rather than simply using Buchanan as a thoroughfare. Referring to the fountains' *origami* design, Asawa said, "It's a deep concept. You take a piece of ordinary, flat piece of paper and make it into a three-dimensional form. If you take that concept and make it out of metal, she said, "you have something that is forever."

"I hope that [Japantown] is a place where I can bring my children, walk them down these streets and point out places where our family lived, where they worked, where they assembled for relocation to the camps, where they were evicted, where I played, where I worked.

All of these places help teach them about their rich heritage, and why it makes them so special, and why they should be proud of their culture. I want them to be able to look at these spots in J-town and nod knowingly, because they clearly understand what it means to be a Japanese American. That is my hope for Japantown."

– Chris Hirano

Originally built in 1968, the 100-foot Peace Pagoda symbolizes the peace, friendship and understanding between the United States and Japan. An effort that began ten years ago to renovate the entire Peace Plaza yields a newly designed, raised plaza and a refurbished pagoda.

A Japanese American Community
Family Photo Album

The Japanese Cultural & Community
Center of Northern California
would like to thank the individuals,
families and businesses that contributed
financially toward the development of
this book. Without their support
and understanding, this project to
preserve the rich history, stories and
personalities of the San Francisco
Japantown community would not have
been possible. The pictures of these
individuals, families and businesses
represent part of the past, present
and future of our ever-changing
community, and we gratefully
acknowledge their participation in
the telling of our story.

The Bank of Tokyo [now the Union Bank of California]
opened Japantown's first bank branch in 1957, on the
corner of Sutter and Buchanan Streets.

Henri & Tomoye Takahashi
and Martha Suzuki.

The first San Francisco account at the Sumitomo Bank of
California [now California Bank & Trust] was opened in
1953, by The National Japanese American Citizen
League

Allen & Pat Okamoto and Family

Bill & May Hirose and Family

Jack & Kiyo Hirose

Barbara Marumoto-Coon & Family

Terry & Sachiko Hatada

Hats & Amey Aizawa

Dick & Jan Yamagami and Family

Mary Kawano and Family

Tanako Hagiwara & Family

Wayne & Sally Osaki and Family

Uta Hirota

Yo Hironaka

Frank & Edith Tanaka and Family

Kitaichi Sakai
(Chieko Sakai) 1920)

Toshiaki Sakaguchi and Family

Carole Hayashino & Kyle Tatsumoto and Family

Dennis & Wendy Shinbori and Family

Ronald & Cynthia Hiura
and Family

Hiko & Susan Shimamoto
and Family

Masako Fukunaga &
Kaz Maniwa and Kenta

George & Alice Oshima

George & Kikuye Kayano

Yosh & June Kitagawa and Family

Kayo Nakamura and
Diane Nakamura

Michi Horio and Family

Jack Nakamura and Family

Yoneo Yoshimura and
Naoko Yoshimura Ito

Jack & Aya Mizono and Family

Kenneth & Yoshiko Ho

Nobusuke & Fumi Fukuda and
Steve

Fred & Irene
Hoshiyama

Henry & Adelina Serata and Family

Minoru & Violet Tanaka

John & Mae Mizono and Family

Nancy Tomioka & Scott Tomioka (Tomioka
family picture circa 1935)

OF THE BOOK PROJECT

Eiko Aoki

Gish & Takako Endo

John & Sue Fong

Sumi Honnami

Paul & Shelly Iwamasa and Family

Gary & Arleen Kitahata

Ken & Rosalyn Kiwata

Masako Koga

Robert & Gail Mametsuka and
Family

Eddie & Alice Moriguchi

Hiroshi F. Masuda and
Etsuko J. Masuda

Ella Toshiko Nakabe

George T. Nobori

Nell H. Noguchi

Wallace & Katherine Nunotani

Rose S. Oda

Ken & Kay Onishi

Keith Onishi

Misao Otsuki

Katherine Reyes

Robert & Alicia Sakai

Walter & Harumi Serata

Joe Shintaku

Harry & Lorraine Suzuki

Joanne Shimamoto Tohei

Richard Untalan & Kerry
Onishi and Family

Barbara S. Wada

Yukio & Yasuko Wada

HATS AIZAWA: Born in the heart of Nihonmachi and a partner in Aizawa Furuta Advertising, Aizawa states, "I am very committed to the survival of Japantown."

LORI ARATANI: A graduate of Boston University, Aratani covers education issues for the *San Jose Mercury News.*

KERWIN BERK: Berk is a graduate of the University of Texas at Austin and works as local news editor at the *San Francisco Chronicle.*

DIANNE FUKAMI: San Francisco native Fukami has produced and directed television documentaries on Japanese Americans and is co-authoring a book about Nikkeis on the Peninsula, south of San Francisco.

PHILIP KAN GOTANDA: Gotanda is a playwright and independent filmmaker who works and resides in San Francisco.

ROBERT HANDA: An Emmy Award-winning journalist, Handa works in the South Bay Bureau of KTVU-TV, and has also been a reporter, anchor and producer at other local stations.

EDWARD IWATA: Iwata is tech writer for *USA Today,* out of the Palo Alto bureau, and previously was a business writer at the *San Francisco Examiner.*

KEN KASHIWAHARA: Kashiwahara is a former television news correspondent reporting international, national and local stories for 30 years. He retired in 1998.

DONNA KATO: A journalist for the *San Jose Mercury News,* Kato was co-president of the local Asian American Journalists Association chapter in 2000. Her grandmother Yuki Kato was a longtime resident of Japantown.

GARY KAWAGUCHI: Kawaguchi, who has a doctorate in Ethnic Studies from UC Berkeley, is Project Director for the Global Diasporas in Southern California, at California State Dominguez Hills.

DANA KAWAOKA: A Yonsei activist, Kawaoka earned her BA in American Studies and Visual Art from UC Santa Cruz.

TED KURIHARA: Originally from Hawai'i, Kurihara is a San Francisco-based commercial photograher. He established his business in 1969.

PAUL KURODA: Kuroda runs a photo stock business through Workbook.com. Previously, he worked as photojournalist and won a National Newspaper Photographer of the Year award.

ROBERT MIZONO: San Francisco native Mizono has photographed for major American, European and Japanese commercial clients and has won numerous awards for his location and portraiture work.

SHEILA MUTO: Muto, a Yonsei, works as a reporter for *The Wall Street Journal* in San Francisco.

ANNIE NAKAO: Hawai'i native Nakao has been a metro reporter and feature writer at the *San Francisco Examiner* for the past 20 years. She covers race, culture and community issues.

NANCY OGAMI: After spending 15 years in Los Angeles, Ogami finally returned to the Bay Area in 1997. She is a freelance graphic designer in San Francisco.

KURT OSAKI: Born on Kaua'i, Osaki started Osaki Design in 1993. His clients include the National Football League, National Hockey League, National Basketball Association and the University of Hawai'i.

PAUL OSAKI: JCCCNC executive director since 1989, Osaki says his parents gave him the "gift to believe in his dreams" and devotes his work on this book to his grandparents, "who first dreamed."

PAUL SAKUMA: Sansei Associated Press photographer Sakuma is president of the SF Bay Area Press Photographers Association and a photojournalism graduate of San Jose State University.

DINA SHEK: A development assistant at San Francisco State University and a board member for the JCCCNC, Shek is working on her masters thesis about Japanese American redress.

BRAD SHIRAKAWA: Shirakawa is a photojournalist, teacher and songwriter based in the South Bay.

JILL SHIRAKI: Interested in drawing upon Nikkei personal stories as avenues for healing and empowerment, Shiraki staffed the Sansei Legacy Project and serves as JCCCNC's program director.

LEA SUZUKI: A recent mother, Suzuki has been a *San Francisco Chronicle* staff photographer for over six years. She has a BA in journalism from San Francisco State University.

DEAN TAKAHASHI: Takahashi works as a staff writer covering technology for the San Francisco bureau of *The Wall Street Journal.* He is a Sansei from Sacramento.

DORI TAKESHITA: Takeshita, who has a strong food background, grew up within J-town, going from JCYC to Konko Church, working at Iroha and Mifune Restaurants, and being an Enchantee.

JOHN TATEISHI: California native Tateishi directed the Japanese American Citizens League's redress campaign and is now the group's national director. He is also principal partner in Tateishi/Shinoda and Associates.

WENDY TOKUDA: Tokuda anchors the evening news for *KRON-TV* (San Francisco). Previously, she anchored and reported for *KNBC* (Los Angeles) and for 14 years at *KPIX* (San Francisco).

KAZUHIRO TSURUTA: Tsuruta has worked as the *SF Asian Art Museum* photographer since 1988. Before that, he was a commercial photographer in San Francisco.

PATTY WADA: Currently employed by the Japanese American Citizens League, Wada has served on the boards of JCCCNC, Kimochi, Inc., Nihonmachi Little Friends and the Japanese AIDS Project.

RICH WADA: Wada is a freelance San Francisco photographer who has been active with community arts groups, including Japantown Art and Media and Kearny Street Workshop.

PATTY WAKIDA: A Yonsei writer and researcher for Heyday books, Wakida is also co-editing an anthology of literature from and about Japanese American internment.

DIANE YEN-MEI WONG: A San Francisco-based freelance writer and editor, Wong writes a column for *Hawaii Herald* newspaper and is working on her next play.

JAN YANEHIRO: Yanehiro was founding co-host of KPIX-TV's "Evening Magazine" from 1976 to 1990, serves on the boards of several groups and hosts programs on *KCSM* (San Mateo) and Home and Garden TV.

SANDRA YOSHIZUKA: A Yonsei from San Jose and a UC Berkeley graduate, Yoshizuka has worked with the Asian American Journalists Association and the National Asian American Telecommunications Association.

CREDITS AND ACKNOWLEDGMENTS

RESOURCE CONTRIBUTORS

Sumi Akashi
Benkyodo
Christ United
    Presbyterian Church
Koyuki and Kenjiro
    Hedani
Yo Hironaka
Fred Hoshiyama
Stephen Ihara
Ken Ina
Jikei-Kai
Sakae and Mitsuko
    Kawashiri
Yuri Kodani
Konko Church of
    San Francisco
Shig Miyamoto
May Murata
National Japanese
    American Historical
    Society
Nichi Bei Times
Okamura Family
Kaoru Okubo
Teresa Ono
Daisy Satoda
San Francisco Flower
    Market
Dennis Shinbori
June Sugihara
Haruo Yokota

PROJECT CONSULTANTS

Gary Kawaguchi
Seizo Oka

PHOTO CONTRIBUTORS

Kinu Abe Matsumoto
Hatsuro Aizawa
The Bancroft Library
Buddhist Church
    of San Francisco
California Department of
    Parks and Recreation
Nob Fukuda
Hagiwara Family
Louise Hanford
Carole Hayashino
Hokubei Mainichi
Sumi Honnami
Momoru Inouye
Motomu Ishii
Japanese American
    Historical Archives
Japanese Community
    Youth Council
Japantown Art
    and Media
Kataoka Family
Kimochi, Inc.
Tsuyako Kitashima
Donna Kotake
Chiz Miyazaki Shiro
Koji Murata
Kerry Nakagawa

Japanese American
    National Library
National Japanese
    American Historical
    Society
Nisei Fishing Club
Michi Onuma
Keiji Okuda
Aiko Onodera
Wayne Osaki
Pine United
    Methodist Church
San Francisco
    Redevelopment Agency
Walter Serata
San Francisco
    Public Library
San Francisco Taiko Dojo
Hiko Shimamoto
Carol Sugimura
Kenji & Sumako Takeshita
Don Tamaki
Frank Tanaka
Isao Tanaka
Johnny Taniguchi
Dave Tatsuno
Richard Wada
Yoneo Yoshimura

RESOURCE TEAM

Nob Fukuda
Carole Hayashino
Yo Hironaka
Lewis Kawahara
Gail Mametsuka
Lori Matoba
Nihonmachi
    Little Friends
Nobiru-Kai
Rumi Okabe
Allen Okamoto
Kathy Reyes
June Sugihara
Carol Sugimura
Kenji Taguma
Tomoye Takahashi
Edith Tanaka
Grant Tomioka
JK Yamamoto

SPECIAL THANKS

Eiko Aoki
The Densho Project
Marjorie Fletcher
Mike Furutani
Ruby Hata
Japanese American
    National Library
Ken Maeshiro
Kaz Maniwa
Cary Matsumura
Jack Matsuoka
Jim Nagareda
Allen Okamoto
Dan Oshima
Sandra Yoshizuka

VOLUNTEERS

Kristin Honma
Karen Nunotani Kern
Nozomi Okabe
Kara Okamoto
Harumi Serata
Sumako Takeshita
Edith Tanaka
Karina Umehara
Chris Wong

WRITING & PHOTO CREDITS